A WHEEL OF SMALL GODS

To Jessie,
who dreams better worlds into being
and gives good ideas freely:
my deepest gratitude and
love without end,
you wonder.

A WHEEL
OF SMALL GODS

POETRY
BRIAN WILKINS

ART
BRENNEN REECE

REVELORE
OLYMPIA, WA ☉ MMXXII

A Wheel of Small Gods
© Brian Wilkins & Brennen Reece 2022

All rights reserved. No part of this publication may be reproduced or utilized in any form or by any means, electronic or mechanical, including photocopying, recording, or by any information storage and retrieval system, without permission in writing from the publishers. The information contained herein is for interest only and does not constitute medical advice.

Book design by Brennen Reece & Jenn Zahrt.
Cover design and all art by Brennen Reece.

Publisher's Cataloging-in-Publication (Provided by Cassidy Cataloguing Services, Inc.).
Names: Wilkins, Brian, 1982- author. | Reece, Brennen, illustrator.
Title: A wheel of small gods / poetry, Brian Wilkins ; art, Brennen Reece.
Description: Olympia, WA : Revelore, [2022] | Includes bibliographical references.
Identifiers: ISBN: 978-1-947544-36-9 (hardback) | 978-1-947544-37-6 (paperback)
Subjects: LCSH: Astrology, Egyptian--Poetry. | Astrology, Egyptian--Pictorial works. | Medicine, Magic, mystic, and spagiric--Poetry. | Medicine, Magic, mystic, and spagiric--Pictorial works. | Healing--Poetry. | Healing--Pictorial works. | Mind and body--Poetry. | Mind and body-- Pictorial works. | LCGFT: Poetry. | BISAC: POETRY / American / General. | BODY, MIND & SPIRIT / Healing / General. | BODY, MIND & SPIRIT / Astrology / General.
Classification: LCC: BF1714.E39 W55 2022 | DDC: 133.59232--dc23

ISBN: 978-1-947544-36-9

Printed worldwide through Ingram.

Revelore Press
1910 East 4th Avenue PMB 141
Olympia, WA 98506
United States

www.revelore.press

First printed in 2022.

CONTENTS

Introduction:
- A Continuum of Care 1
- Ritual Healing 4
- Spirits and Sickness 7
- The Wheel of Small Gods 10
- Theory 12
- Practice 16

Poems:
- CANCER II: Somachalmais: Lungs 21
- CANCER III: Charmine: Spleen 23
- LEO I: Zoloias: Heart 25
- LEO II: Zachor: Upper Back 27
- LEO III: Frich : Liver 29
- REGULUS: Raphael 31
- VIRGO I: Zamendres: Belly 33
- VIRGO II: Magois: Bowels 35
- VIRGO III: Michulais: Navel 37
- LIBRA I: Psineus: Buttocks & Rectum 39
- LIBRA II: Chusthisis: Urethra, Bladder, & Urinary Tract 41
- LIBRA III: Psamiatois: Anus 43
- SCORPIO I: Necbeuos: Clitoris & Penis 45
- SCORPIO II: Turmantis: Genitals 47
- SCORPIO III: Psermes: Reproductive Organs 49
- ANTARES: Uriel 51

SAGITTARIUS I: Clinothois: Thigh Sores	53
SAGITTARIUS II: Thursois: Bones	55
SAGITTARIUS III: Renethis: Thighs	57
CAPRICORN I: Renepois: Kneecaps	59
CAPRICORN II: Manethois: Back of the Knees	61
CAPRICORN III: Marxois: Knees	63
AQUARIUS I: Ularis: Shins	65
AQUARIUS II: Luxois: Fatty Tissue of the Legs	67
AQUARIUS III: Crauxes: Leg Muscles	69
FOMALHAUT: Gabriel	71
PISCES I: Fambrais: Abscesses of the Feet	73
PISCES II: Flugmois: Infections of the Feet	75
PISCES III: Piastris: The Feet	77
ARIES I: Aulathamus: The Head	79
ARIES II: Sabaoth: Temples & Nose	81
ARIES III: Disornafias: Ears, Uvula, & Teeth	83
TAURUS I: Jaus: The Neck	85
TAURUS II: Sarnatois: Tonsils & Tongue	87
TAURUS III: Romenur: Mouth & Throat	89
CAPUT ALGOL: The Demon's Head	91
ALDEBARAN: Michael	93
GEMINI I: Manuchos: Shoulders	95
GEMINI II: Samurois: Arms	97
GEMINI III: Azuel: Hands	99
CANCER I: Sotheir: Sides of the Trunk	101

ACKNOWLEDGEMENTS

Brian

I would like to offer my sincere thanks to the following folks:

Jess Waters, for her impeccable ear, for her unfailing support, and for always being right. This book would not exist without you.

Brennen Reece, for bringing decans into incredible visible appearance.

Gordon White, for introducing me to these spirits and for his friendship, even if he has to live on faraway Goth Island.

Mark Goszytla, Sarah Stickney, and M. R. B. Chelko for encouraging early drafts and being earnest friends.

Jenn Zahrt, for wanting weird books out in the world and making them happen.

To my family for believing poetry is a good idea.

To all my Soupers, who have always made me feel like "ONE OF US. ONE OF US."

And to the spirits, both in this book and without, who work wonders tirelessly for the benefit of all.

Brennen

Parker, for whom I am everything I am, for whom I do everything I do.

Lisa, for unconditional support and tolerating my constant rambling on about the strangest things.

My mother and grandmother, who raised me in a magical universe.

Andy, Alan, Randy, Jason, and Chris, for encouraging my love of beautiful nonsense.

Brian and Jenn, for the opportunity, as well as their unending patience.

Gordon, whom I know mainly through his words, a light in the darkness and path through the forest, and without whom I would have never met Brian.

INTRODUCTION

For the first few years of my son's life, nothing scared me more than his asthma. The wrong sort of wheeze meant a trip to the emergency room. The rasping, panting, rattling sound of it, coupled with a pneumatic cough, still haunts my nightmares. In dark hospital rooms while my son slept and the pulse-ox monitor clipped along, I would practice gratitude—gratitude to doctors, to nurses, to oxygen treatment, to medicines, to prayers, to St. Guinefort who watches over sick children. It was what I could do.

And I found myself saying gratefully an all-too-common phrase: "I'm so glad we don't live 100 years ago." It would crop up in conversations and people would nod sagely. But the question began to bother me: what would I have done to save my son 100 years ago?

The problem with being interested in history is that this is the sort of thing that keeps you up at night. If you know the shape of the past—collapsed civilizations and forgotten languages—it's clear that the conditions of 100 years ago are never that far away from your own future.

What we imagine shapes what we can do. And yes, 90 years ago when asthma was considered a psychological issue best handled by "the talking cure," he would have been much worse off.[1] But 1900 years ago, in the Greco-Roman cities dotting the Mediterranean, he would have received medical care to rival our present standards.

A Continuum of Care

Antibiotics, sanitation, diagnostics, anesthesia, a well-mapped understanding of the circulatory and nervous system: all of those elements of modern medicine are present in classical medicine.

Classical and medieval handbooks include complicated recipes for antibiotics that can kill staph infections. Clean water was the hallmark of the Roman city. Doctors used many different diagnostic methods including observing the chemical changes on plants and animals when exposed to samples taken from a patient. Anesthesia of various kinds was used by Roman surgeons across the breadth of the Empire. And the complicated ethics of vivisection paved the way for modern neuroscience through the work of Erasistratus and Herophilos, with their distinction of the cerebrum and cerebellum, as well as the description of the different layers of the eye—in 300 BC.

The change comes from the ability to distribute those elements evenly. That is not an economic argument. City states in Greece often provided public doctors, and doctors were expected to be charitable to the poor as a part of their training. But transport and storage were significant challenges.

Even if you've never rushed a gasping child to the hospital, I hope you'll feel my deep appreciation for the car. No one had to ride a horse to fetch the doctor, wait for him to rouse from his laudanum stupor to hitch his wagon, and then drive a team of horses back to our house to then begin his diagnosis. Hopefully he would have had the proper medicines in supply and be able to transport them.

These remain issues in rural America—not the horses, but limited doctors, medicines, and ambulances. More to the point, if I hadn't been able to drive my son to the hospital his health would have been in a much more precarious place. And if they had not had a shelf stable supply of the interventions he needed, his chances would have also decreased. These are issues of access, rather than a contrast in ability to treat.

What did the doctors do to save my son? They provided supplemental oxygen, anti-inflammatories, steroids, and depending on the tests, an antibiotic. He was also given home steroids and an albuterol nebulizer. I am not arguing against these as improvements. Each of these interventions should be seen as on a continuum from the work of Hellenistic doctors, not as somehow separate from that history. We have these elements *because* of the classical period, not despite it. But I am writing about what we've lost. That's what haunts me about history: what we forget, and what that means for our chance to imagine a better future.

For example, Galen of Pergamum (129–210 AD) and others identified asthma as a problem of muscular spasms and were capable of prescribing inhaled stramonium (an anticholinergic compound with analogs used in inhalers today) for relaxing the lungs. By 77 AD, Pliny the Elder recommended the use of Ephedra mixed in red wine—a herbal version of applied epinephrine. Again, are there advantages to modern medicines in these regards? In a lot of cases, yes, but we're not looking at a sea change in treatment but improvements of existing concepts. Sit with that for a second. My son would have received medicinal treatment from the same family of plants in 327 BC as he does now.

It's worth a comparison of the two situations. Imagine, for a moment, that my son and I were in Pergamum—the rival to Alexandria in every way—in 157 AD. From the statue of Athena in the library (second largest in the world), it was a little over two miles to the temple of Asclepius, god of medicine and healing.

There are good arguments the image relates to the practice of drawing hookworms from the body by curling them around a stick. See also the Nehushtan referenced in 2 Kings 18:4 and Numbers 21:4-9 — the bronze serpent on a staff through which Moses healed.

Asclepius is the son of Apollo, tutored by the centaur Chiron in medicine. In one version of the myth, he performs an act of kindness to a snake, who whispers the secrets of healing in his ears. The snake joined him, curling around his staff, hence the symbol of medicine we know today.

The Asclepion served many of the same functions as a modern hospital. It was centered on a sacred spring, and included not only housing for pilgrims and staff, but also the abaton (the place for encountering Asclepius in dreams), an amphitheater, a theater, and a library. Like all the temples to Asclepius, it was a beautiful spot apart from the city and here the priests and attendants of Asclepius would care for the sick.

First, we would have been escorted past a wall where past cures were carved in stone, and offerings left to Asclepius in the form of statues of healed body parts, poems, and other images of success. We might even have caught sight of Galen practicing surgery on wounded gladiators. Once inside the building, my son would be given a purifying bath, and then clean white robes to wear. A priest (probably a doctor, as they often made up the priesthood of Asclepius) would hear his symptoms, including details about his diet and lifestyle.[2] Then he would have been given a room to sleep in so that the god could visit in dream and offer a cure. Once he had a dream, he would discuss it with the priest again, who would interpret it and offer recommendations. It was particularly favorable to dream of a dog or snake licking your wounds.

The doctor/priest would prescribe what we would think of as medical interventions: herbal compounds, dietary advice, and some sort of physical therapy. In addition, they would make

Therapeutae, the term for the attendants of the god, and of course the origin of therapeutic.

In Galen's tenure tending the gladiators, only 5 died. 60 died during his predecessor's term. But he wasn't fooling around, referring to wounds as "windows to the body" and getting the job by eviscerating an ape, challenging the other doctors to fix it, and then doing it himself.

recommendations for actions to fulfill the will of the god, which could just be the medical treatment put forward or it could also include pilgrimages, prayers, magic, and the contemplation of images, poems, or music. And then we would be trundled home if we were ready to follow the treatment plan.

I'm going to return in a minute to the question of spiritual intervention, but for the moment, consider this comparison. My son's treatment at the hospital included many attendants: a pediatrician, a pulmonologist, a dietician, 24-hour nursing, and a social worker. He was prescribed medicines, dietary advice, recommendations for his physical health, and while he did not have his dreams interpreted by anyone but me, the nurses brought him talismanic objects at every visit he had: a handmade pillow case, a teddy bear, an Easter basket.

In short, materialist medicine has arrived at the same pattern of treatment presented by the priests of Asclepius in the time of Marcus Aurelius, though it has lost one key element...

Magic.

Ritual Healing

Because doctors no longer acknowledge the role of the imaginal in our health, despite studies designed by their own criteria to understand it, our healing paradigm is incomplete. First, it's important to understand that, as Lionell Snell puts it, "Placebo has become the politically correct term for magical healing."[3] While I do think that magical healing encompasses more than just what is covered by placebo, they overlap in key areas: consciousness effects brought on by using imagination and ritual to heal patients.

No serious study of a painkiller, for example, will take place without a double-blind test involving a placebo (commonly understood as an inert substance). However, a 2015 study in *PAIN: The Journal for the International Association for the Study of Pain* found that new painkillers had a limited advantage coming to market because the effect of placebo was growing in US patients with neuropathic pain.[4]

In other words, the ritual of providing a pill and suggesting that it works is becoming *more effective* over time, to *rival* the new drugs. The imagination, properly deployed, is providing pain relief on its own.

Imagining requires bringing into being a reality in which healing is possible and accomplished. This part can be very hard to grasp because it eliminates a strict material understanding of reality very quickly. Chemical processes in your body, as well as the physical structure of your brain, respond to verbal stimuli. This means that there is no mind/body split, but rather a spectrum. What we commonly think of as material is mutable and alive, while what we characterize as "just a thought" can have concrete and immediate physical effects.

Over time the definition of placebo (and its negative cousin, nocebo) has changed from just an inert substance to the entire psychosocial context surrounding the patient and the effect of this context has on the patient's experience, brain, and body.[5]

Studies looking at placebo have found reductions in pain, enhancements of effects, and increased ability to create desired outcomes.[6] Kissing it does actually make it better. Placebo also has positive effects on the immune system,[7] including reducing the common cold.[8] My absolute favorite study on how thoughts are causative was conducted by Alia Crum and William Corbin, and it is the best not only because it's a clear example but also because it involves milkshakes.[9]

Crum and Corbin collected participants for an experiment ostensibly about the different nutrient contents of two milkshakes. They said they wanted to measure the metabolic effects of each one. One was presented as an indulgent, 620-calorie shake and the other as a low-fat, 140-calorie shake. The participants were told they were comparing for taste.

However, both sets of participants were offered the same 380-calorie shake with different labels. The result? When participants enjoyed their indulgent shake, their ghrelin levels declined sharply. Sensible shake? Remained about the same. Ghrelin, often called the hunger hormone, decreases when you are satiated.

Sit with it. The label of the milkshake and the subsequent expectation of outcome changed the production of the hormone in the body. Not only that, it matched the expected outcome of eating a high-calorie food. Regardless of calories, the body responded physically as if the high-calorie food had been eaten.

Thinking you are eating "healthy food" that is "sensible" will not, in fact, satisfy you despite its physical properties.

But these imaginative effects are not limited to helping. A recent review of the ethical implications of nocebo points out that while words are powerful tools for doctors, they are "…two-edged swords that can maim or heal."[10] Well, actually, I want to quibble there. Two-edged swords don't do much healing. It's better to think of the magic doctors do as a hammer.

Or, frankly, cursing.

For example, Häuser *et. al.* show that the adverse side effects of medication depend on the expectations of patients and doctors (2012). The expectation itself can generate side effects even in sham trials—meaning that nothing but a sugar pill and the information about side effects was given to the patient, but the patient experienced the side effects all the same.

Symptoms can also be caused by suggestion. For example, 26% of people given a sugar pill supposedly containing lactose, who have no previous lactose intolerance, experience gastrointestinal distress. Suggesting that lactose can cause those symptoms led to the patient experiencing them.[11]

This experience is so widespread that there is now a debate regarding the ethics of briefing patients on side effects. Various organizations insist that proper phrasing to avoid nocebo effects is part of a physician's duty of care.[12]

To explain the mechanism behind these effects (and I do recommend you read the papers, they are fascinating), researchers trace the various biological pathways affected. That's a good thing to know, but unless it adds information on how to generate or avoid these effects, it's just an academic exercise. It doesn't explain *why* this might be the case. The strict materialist worldview cannot explain it. I do applaud all the researchers changing their model of the world in face of the data.

While placebo research shows pretty amazing effects, the research on prayer is muddier. In part, this is because regulating what counts as "healing prayer" is very difficult to do under lab conditions. Also, very few people are interested in the idea of effective prayer. It's a jump already to try to test these ideas, and then no one wants to tell people their beliefs don't work.

I think beliefs are irrelevant. It's the method that more often fails with prayer, and we can extrapolate that from the placebo research.

This is quite possibly true of a wider range of prayers, but the contemporary American Protestant Christian context is what I am most familiar with and exemplifies the issue well.

A lot of American Protestant Christian prayer injects fear and worry into the patient. For example, if you look closely at the guidelines for avoiding nocebo effects with doctors, you'll note the recommendations explicitly mention causing uncertainty. "This medication may help" damages its ability to help. But most prayers offered in a contemporary Christian context embed this idea of failure in the actual phrasing of the prayer itself. It's all too common to hear "If it is your will, Lord, please heal X." And there we go: it may not be God's will. I would argue that whether it is or not is none of your business.

It is interesting that this does not match the method of healing prayer in the gospels. Christ almost entirely uses the imperative:

stand and walk, wake up, be healed, etc. Peter continues the same in Acts with his healing of the lame beggar, though adding the authority of the name of Jesus. Doubt is not invoked. In fact, faith in the outcome is often listed as the main prerequisite of healing.

So why do people waver in their prayers? Because they're afraid, no matter what their cosmology, of failing. Or that their god will fail. The choices seem to be: that God chooses not to heal, and is uncaring; that God fails to heal and is not omnipotent; that we fail to heal, and are now responsible. And none of those ideas sound particularly attractive. Yet this is the sort of dilemma doctors face, and their answer is to bring all of their skill to bear to help the patient.

If instead of a predetermined outcome that may be fixed by pleading, what if prayer functioned like other interventions—meaning, it added an increased probability of success? This is exactly what placebo healing does when used properly: it offers an increased chance the patient will recover, and recover more quickly with less pain. Sometimes the results of that imaginative integration are incredibly swift; more often, like the more common miracles of birth and growth, they happen in slow and wonderful ways.

And since this approach to healing does work, it benefits us to examine the cultures, current and historical, that used placebo to great effect. And one of the primary ways that magic engages with illness is to approach it as a spirit.

Spirits and Sickness

This is a book of magic, and as such it takes the existence of spirits, their ability to influence the world, and the human capacity to influence them as a given. This understanding is based on my personal interactions and my listening to many other and older cultures who maintain the truth of these ideas. Material reality as it is imagined by the New Atheists is a theory which fails over and again to explain things it cannot conceive, and therefore dismisses them as unreal.

Like, for instance, the imagination. Try building a bridge without imagining it first. Reality is a spectrum of incarnation. We know, for example, that imagining navigating a maze activates the same areas of the brain as walking it. The idea of the maze is made physical in the brain. And we communicate ideas to each other through metaphor: the speaking of which also engages the same physical process, if it's done well. To communicate as a human with an idea requires the imagination.

The imagination is many things, one of which seems to be the place where we interact with spirits. This leaves the question of what is a spirit. I see them as a person that represents a concept and has a life of their own that can act and relate with other persons. Trees have individual spirits reflected in their own particular story. But they also participate in the spirit of the forest, and of their lineage of trees. In the same way, humans have a spirit and a physical lineage, as well as being a part of all things human.

But there are spirits not currently within the body as well.

Imagine a dancer: beautiful, strong, and waiting. They are about to converse with the spirit of a dance. The dance has its own body and component parts. First, rhythm: whether drums or claps or the dancer's own beating heart. But a rhythm permeates it. Then the steps, whether established or improvised. The dancer joins the rhythm, engages with the steps, but this may still not be *dancing*. The meaning behind the movements, the art of it all, may not yet be present. The dancer merges with the presence of the dance, and then it becomes clear to everyone watching. They're moved, feel the need to dance along, feel the emotion rippling through them. And then the dance is made real.

This is not something radical. And people can try to explain what spirit is in all sorts of ways, but the truth is we recognize it when it is present. We know it also by its absence. Rhythm is not spirit. The steps are not spirit. The intention of the artist is not spirit, either: it lives in the unity of these things.

Animism, a catchall term for ways of living that approach all living things as having personhood, allows you to encounter these spirits. Anything that has a story is a person and can be communicated with.

The same can be said of illness. In the Hellenistic context, illness was conceived of as both having a spirit and there being spirits that could cause illness. The distinction isn't as clear as we would make now. And the spirits that controlled illness, like the god Apollo, could both give it as a punishment or stave it off.

This concept is not unique to the syncretized culture of the Roman Empire. While it's important to be careful in comparison, and we cannot say that the viewpoints of Hellenistic magicians are the same as those of Aboriginal Australian groups, we can put them next to each other and note where there is overlap. Aboriginal culture is at least 50,000 years old, and it is probable it serves as an example of far older human history.

In *Journey into Dreamtime*, Munya Andrews provides some explanations of how sickness works in an Aboriginal context.[13]

She explains a concept called "sickness dreaming." A "dreaming" encompasses a way in which people understand the world, live in it, have gifts and obligations from it, to it, and with it, and what they also express as they live. It is not a dream which happens in sleep, but is a Creation Time that is ongoing.[14] It is the story of a life and how it fits in with all the other parts of the network of the living.

Places and people can have sickness dreaming, while illnesses have their own dreamings, too. When someone visits a place that is sickness country, it can make them ill or even kill them if they don't have the proper cultural protections. The taboos and ritual practices surrounding sickness country maintain a right relationship to it.

For example, some of these sickness places exist where there are high levels of uranium deposits. From a materialist point of view, the physical presence of the uranium explains sickness country, but it is far more subtle than that. If you stay too long in these places, or don't respect the cultural protections you need to survive, you may become very sick. But *some people* also have immunity to this sort of sickness because of a kin relationship to the land. In other words, the uranium is an aspect of the spirit of the place that *can* make you sick depending on your relationship to it. But also that understanding how the dreaming of the country functions can keep you safe.

Personal dreamings (or family and clan dreamings) of sickness provide immunity to certain kinds of illness. The person has a deeper understanding of the kind of illness and can even be an expert in healing it. As Andrews explains, healing is not quite the right concept. Because the illness understands the human as being a part of them, they don't affect the human. And then humans understand how to relate to the illness.

Perhaps the most relevant part to our Pergamene adventure is that sickness isn't something that you battle: it's a lesson and a friend come to teach. Rather than fight off an illness, you sit with it and learn from it. And that process is what true healing entails.

This is not to say that a disease is the fault of the person who engages with it, nor am I saying that in any sense anyone deserves suffering. It's no one's fault they have asthma. But a better understanding of the causes of asthma and how to interact with them, with its spirit, will help reduce suffering.

In the Fall of 2019, I had one of the worst cases of flu I've experienced in my life. For ten days I left my bed to get water and that was about it. And during that time, particularly when my fever was spiking, I had an incredible dream about bees—that every thought in my head was its own bee, and that the hive was my consciousness. Rather than accept the flow of the hive as a single concept, I tried to keep track of every bee (I know, I'm a genius). And it was driving me crazy. It was only after I stopped doing that in dream that my fever broke and I began to recover. I have tried to hold on to that lesson.

The Wheel of Small Gods

Communicating with spirits was normal across the classical world. Asclepius offered wisdom on how to exorcise spirits (which means to command, not to drive out) or engage with them in various ways to heal illness, including making offerings and pilgrimages. But the visit to the Asclepion was only one way to engage with these concepts. Hermetic thinking offered many different ways to talk with the spirits, but the *The Sacred Book of Hermes to Asclepius* (SBHA) provides a standard method: creating an image of the spirit combined with an incantation and a plant ally.[15] It's unlikely this was offered separate to other medical interventions. It was a part of them.

That approach to thinking commonly reflected in Hellenistic culture and centering around the mythical teacher Hermes Trismegistus.

It's not a surprise that the book is attributed as letter from Hermes to Asclepius: this is a passing on of divine knowledge from one god of healing to another. The SBHA is a Romano-Greco-Egyptian document that works in a different cosmology than the sickness dreaming explained by Munya Andrews. Even with that in mind, the similarities are striking.

The SBHA communicates with spirits of time. In Egypt, the year was 360 days, with five intercalary festival days to fit the solar rotation. The year was further divided into 36 ten-day periods, later called decans by the Greeks. Each of these decans was associated with a particular god that ruled not just the time of the year, but certain plants and illnesses. They were also associated with the rising of certain stars. This "wheel of small gods" established the calendar and functioned as a sort of almanac.

The best quick history on the subject is Austin Coppock's 36 Faces: The History, Astrology, and Magic of the Decans (Three Hands Press, 2014). A new edition of this out-of-print text is set to appear any day now.

But by the time of Hellenistic Greece, the stars no longer appeared in the same part of the sky. Precession, the process by which the sun appears to move to different places relative to the stars due to the orbit of the Earth, meant that every 72 years would result in a visible change. Rather than continuing to update which stars signaled the decan, Hellenistic astrologers divided the zodiac itself into 36 divisions: three for each of the twelve signs.

This concept is true to their original nature as calendar gods—they are spirits of time, rather than being the spirit of a star.

And the division of the year continued in the same way. This also gave the decans a position of primacy: they were beyond the stars, and so could influence events in a very powerful way, according to the astrology of the moment.

Each of the decans rules a third of a sign of the zodiac. Each decan has a name (or many names, as people have called them various things over time) and can also be called by its location in the zodiac. It is possible to identify a decan as Sagittarius I, Clinothois—time and one of its names. And these named spirits can be communicated with.

The SBHA attributes each of the decans an image and rulership of part of the body. If a person is afflicted by illness in this area, they are to construct a ring with the image and its name engraved on it, set in metal (sometimes prescribed) over a plant related to that illness/decan, and impose a certain dietary taboo. Many of the plants involved have a direct connection to medicine used to treat that particular illness today.

In other documents relating to the decans, it's clear that these spirits are in command of these afflictions, and may both inflict or remove them. They have these illnesses—they possess them and are them. But the illness in the person is a sign that a relationship with the decan exists and must be navigated. Right relationship is restored through communication.

The ring provides a place in which those negotiations can take place. There is no distinction between the image and its spirit. It's best to think of it as a fractal representation of the larger spirit—contact is made through the interaction with the image. In fact, the image is the preserved method of understanding the nature of these spirits. While the descriptions shift based on different cultures, as do the names, the images are always an attempt to represent the nature of a particular spirit—its functions and personality.

Here we can see the similarity with the Australian Aboriginal sickness dreaming: in both cases, there is a story/spirit that humans can interact with. If your child has asthma, you would communicate with the second decan of the sign Cancer, named Ouphisit, who appears as a woman with the body of a bird with her wings outstretched, about to take flight. Engraved on green jasper with a night-blooming plant beneath it, the spirit can be invoked to protect against diseases of the lungs. And during that time, the patient has to avoid food that a dog has touched.

An image that serves as story. Requirements of ritual action. Respecting certain taboos. These elements allow for imaginative interaction with the spirit. That interaction creates a place for negotiating right relationship and overall healing. These ideas sprung from a particular culture and are deeply entwined with it. Our version may look different but putting this layer of imaginative healing back in its context is essential to improving our outcomes.

Classical medicine understood this concept—it is a post-enlightenment change to leave it unconsidered. Which is why, after a chat about asthma, a trip to see a snake god, an attempt to pin down spirits, and a rundown of placebo research I can actually tell you what is in this book of poems and drawings.

It's medicine.

Theory

I was inspired to begin this project by Gordon White: a chaos magician, writer, podcaster, and driving force behind getting people from Western cultures to treat animism seriously. He started an online membership site called Rune Soup for folks looking to, in his words, re-enchant the world.[16]

In 2017, Gordon offered the members an experiment: what would happen if we engaged in a ritual to connect to the 36 decan spirits over the course of the year? The general goal was contact. I am not going to share with you that ritual nor the results of that experiment: I encourage you to join Rune Soup and give it a whirl. But I will share what happened to me, and what I experienced.

A year long ritual changes how you see time. Add in dealing with time spirits, and it gets even more intense. My process involved some visualization, and through active imagination I could talk to these spirits. But the spirits become a part of your mundane life, not just limited to ritual. The more I conversed with them, the more I understood that they could really help with illness. And they *wanted* to.

Active imagination is a Jungian technique. In effect you enter a daydream state and maintain a feeling of engaging with the dream itself. You're conscious, but the responses the dream figures offer you are often wild and unpredictable. It's immensely useful as a therapy and for talking to spirits.

I was conversing with the spirit of SAGITTARIUS II, Thursois, in ritual. If you're curious about what it's like, I can only tell you what it's like for me: I could feel and see the figure in my mind's eye. He had the face of a weasel and the body of a man. I would always ask these spirits for conversation, and in this case, he was pissed. Well, hurt and offended. Thursois regulates bonesetting, and he kept pointing at my big toe. I had it broken for me (karate tournament) almost 18 years before. He asked why I hadn't called on him to fix it. I said I didn't know about him then. He sniffed and huffed and said that didn't matter.

The next day a friend of mine sent me an email. She was very upset. She manages her mental health through running and had broken her big toe. She's used to foot injuries, and while she had an appointment to get it confirmed by the doctor, she said she was sure it was broken. She wasn't sure how she was going to make it through the winter if she couldn't run.

With the spirit's words still in my head, and with my friend's permission, I decided to see if I could heal her broken toe with decan magic. I drew out the image, wrote out the name, drew the plant in question, and asked for the outcome I wanted. The procedure wasn't quite right, so I spoke an extemporaneous poem over it. Then it felt right, and I sent her a picture of it (as well as the drawing, eventually) and wished her well. I didn't think about it after I did it.

She called me after her doctor's appointment. The toe wasn't broken. She said she couldn't understand it. She was happy it was just a little strain, but she was adamant that the injury had been far worse. She said it was like she healed up really quickly. She lost almost no time in her practice and had time to think about other important ways to protect her mental health if she did get injured.

Something people who don't practice magic often assume is that doing something like this means you do it all the time. It doesn't. There are moments that flare up where magic becomes a good option, and you do it then. Sure, there's meditation and movement and divination and prayer and altars. But this sort of thing isn't a daily event.

Even so, I began to realize that I was finding something important by engaging with these spirits. I began to research the plants and the ways of healing. But more than anything else, I wanted to meet them in the way that my art and imagination connects most.

I am not a visual artist, but I love poetry. Poems are gateways for me. They bring the reader the chance to step through the words into a dream. Art is a kind of magic. It can serve as a way to connect to spirits and the spirit itself. Art is the accessible edge of ritual. A novel can cause you to drop your day job and seek enlightenment in India. A painting may haunt you for a year. A song can make you fall in love. We know this is true, but we treat it like a minor thing. I am asking you to ask yourself: what if it isn't? What if the expression of imagined ideas is one of the most powerful experiences in your life?

Poetry in particular is well suited to magic because it is not a report of an experience, but a method for activating the experience of someone else within yourself. Where the image may be something you can reproduce on a stone, the poem is the ritual that allows for contact.

I follow the American poet H.D. in the concept that poetry is rarely representative but is better understood as an engine of ecstasy. A poem should induce a trance state. It should bridge your entry to the spirit world, or what H.D. called the "overmind." To paraphrase her from her essay "Notes on Thought and Vision"—my signposts are not yours, but by blazing my own trail I may urge you into your own worlds of discovery.[17] I may be able to introduce you to this wheel of small gods.

It came to me that these 36 spirits wanted me to write a series of poems as a response. So after the first year of doing the ritual, I decided I would spend the next year writing. Mostly, I didn't want to stop talking (this surprises no one). So I decided I would make a three year project: year one was the ritual, year two was writing, year three would be editing.

As I went along, the spirits informed me that the poems would look really great with facing images. So I contacted my friend Brennen Reece and he agreed to sketch the figures to match the poems. Like me, he worked within the timing of the decan, sketching and creating the image in that moment as a type of talisman. Two separate streams of inspiration combined into one.

In addition, as the manuscript developed, it became clear that the 4 Royal Stars and Caput Algol also needed a place as markers of time. The spirits connected with those stars are also present.

But I am in no way the first artist to attempt these works. In this, I want to pay respect to my elders in the Western tradition: the 20th-century surrealist painters Remedios Varo and Leonora Carrington. By examining two of their paintings, we can see how this process plays out.

My magical partner, Jess Waters, who has guided me through learning about Carrington and Varo in the way your cool older cousin slips you music you ought to know about, pointed me to these pieces.[18] Carrington and Varo were very close friends, painters, writers, alchemists, and witches.[19] They experimented with the intersection of art, magic, alchemy, and astrology in their kitchens in Mexico City, creating ways of ritual engagement with the imaginal that should be far more closely studied. Both believed art was alchemy—a form of magic devoted to transformation and the finding of the universal medicine.

Each was commissioned to paint a mural for a hospital and sadly, neither work was completed. But we can see from their sketches what ideas they thought essential to include. In Varo's *Creation of the World (Study for Cancer Pavilion: Microcosm)*, she includes a combination of astrological and alchemical images embodied as beings in order to create an environment of healing.[20] Not to mention Asclepius himself, looking on in the lower left corner.

Varo represents the zodiacal figures of Scorpio, Sagittarius, and Capricorn presiding over the patients of the hospital. As Meredith Derks argues, this is a representation of the alchemical process of separation, incineration, and fermentation: the transmutation process that results in life itself. She also includes a "terrifying vessel," a figure that is shedding disease into the world. And so, again following Derks, we see the transformation of illness into health and life—not a war against illness, but an acceptance and alteration of it, central to the ideas in alchemy.

Carrington took a similar tack in approaching her mural for Mexico City's Oncology Hospital. In one panel, she depicts a doctor and a scientist working together under the influence of the stars. Above them swirl the planets, flanked by images of Cancer and Capricorn. These are likely to represent the solstices and the paths in between life and death, but may also carry much of the same astrological and alchemical significance offered by Varo. Behind the doctors, a woman, possibly a reference to the first alchemist, Mary of Egypt, carries an alchemical flask.

In both cases we see the calling down and representation of stars as figures, presented as the guiding light for aiding in recovery. The ideas of transformation, conversation, and interaction underpin their approach to healing. The works are meant to inspire healing through the connection to the images provided. They transmute the imagination of the viewer through ecstasy. That isn't a representation of alchemy: it *is* alchemy.

Both Varo and Carrington included materials in their paintings to use alchemical methods to convey their ideas. While not exactly the same, it certainly rhymes with the method of the SBHA in combining the related plants with the ideas. This is a physical interaction: your eyes are interacting through the medium of light with the painting. What comes off the painting enters your body through your eyes, in addition to the process of physical imagination mentioned above.

It is interesting that both of these commissions were meant to be murals. They would affect patients as they entered the hospital—much as the collection of cures would have done in the Asclepion. This combination of method and intention with expectation is exactly what I'm attempting to do and an important function of art and magic.

In another interesting point of comparison, Munya Andrews identifies the Rainbow Serpent not only as the spirit connected to the uranium sickness dreaming but as a spirit of rebirth. She then connects it to the Western image of Scorpio as Eagle, seeing the bird-snake combination present in both. This is the sort of fruitful conversation that leads to better understanding.

Practice

And then, my Granddaddy was diagnosed with bladder cancer. He was in his late 90s by this point and suffering from dementia already. The doctors told us that bladder cancer could be extremely painful and hard for him to understand or deal with given the dementia. I knew my Granddaddy was at peace about his life and not afraid of death. But I saw no need for him to spend his last years in pain. And so I asked Brennen if he would sketch Libra III, Chusthois, who has rulership over the bladder, and I sent it to my Granddaddy. My father, a Baptist minister, read him my poem and showed him the image. My dad would describe this as a type of prayer, and I don't at all disagree. I will happily argue with you over coffee about why animism is a better way to approach this topic. But we will do so after we tend to the sick.

The spirits did not heal my Granddaddy of bladder cancer. But he had no pain from it. All through his hospice and till the end of his life he never complained about it. Which to me amounts to a miracle for which I am very grateful.

Again we see the same pattern: we engage in ritual and see the effect of diminished pain—an exact match to what the placebo research offers.

At this point, I understood more about the shape of this project. This wasn't just a chance for some fun art or to play with these images. It's a chance for these spirits, these ideas, to have a way into people's lives. And though I don't know the mechanism, I believe that it can help people.

I want to take a moment to be extremely clear about what I'm claiming to be true. I believe, based on the evidence of history and contemporary science, that it is imperative we engage in ritual imaginative processes, in magic, to better heal ourselves. It is an important part of the understanding of medicine that we have lost. And I think that art is the first place to start with that engagement with ritual. You can contemplate a picture and read a poem. You can believe in the power of that to help you heal. And you should, because it does.

Ritual healing works in the way medicine works: it engages with circumstances that increase your chance to heal. And like medicine, if improperly administered it can hurt. The good news is that the process is simple. Expect healing. You will raise the odds of recovery. The lack of specificity and control with art, the attempt at general uplift, is one of its advantages in many circumstances.

This book is our understanding of the spirits. We make no claims to having any kind of ownership of them: it's a polyamorous affair and there's room for all. You too can have your own relationship with Thursois. But more to the point, what you see here is filtered through our experience—this is a field guide, not channeled material. I am not presenting poems that are the voice of the decan. I am showing you my notes on what I found traveling in that country.

The poems are narrative and imagistic scenes, not invocations in the traditional sense. Rather than call down powers and bind them with formulae composed of angelic names, fumigations, and drawn circles, I am offering a way into an ecstatic state that allows a chance for meeting. I am writing you a letter of introduction to some good friends.

And I do not wish to prescribe a method for your interaction. For instance, The Egyptian year begins with Cancer: my personal engagement with the ritual began in Cancer II, and so I'm presenting the spirits as I encountered them. In addition, I have added the attributions of afflictions from the SBHA to each poem, as a nod to tradition. I am also including a table here for easy reference.

There are some small deviations from traditional attribution, in that there seems to be some repetitions and confusions in the original text. Changes are based on my personal spirit contact and experience.

Some of you may find it easiest to read the poems, contemplate the image, and see what happens. You may find a connection in dream. For some, it may be valuable to try these experiments in the corresponding decan. For others, making your own art to engage with the same spirits will be the best way forward.

When Jenn asked me what the Decans wanted this book to be, I had a vision of sitting in the middle of the poems. I saw myself sending them off to friends in need of healing: postcard talismans, that were both the Asclepion and the offerings around it. And we realized we were talking about an oracle deck, which is available as a companion to this book at *www.revelore.press/wosg*. An oracle is the temple, the spirit, and the message. It is the direct presence of the gods in your life, and while I do hope that this book of poems is that for you as well, it is certainly harder to slip in your pocket and leave with a sick friend.

I hope you find the Decan spirits good company. I hope you feel their presence, and your life changes. More than anything else, I hope you find your own way to bring about healing in your life and the lives of your kin. Because we can help each other, with imagination, a little art, and compassion.

Good luck.

Notes

1. Melissa Opolski and Ian Wilson, "Asthma and Depression: A Pragmatic Review of the Literature and Recommendations for Future Research," *Clinical Practice and Epidemiology in Mental Health* 1.18 (2005): https://www.ncbi.nlm.nih.gov/pmc/articles/PMC1253523/
2. 85% macaroni and cheese, like all children.
3. Lionel Snell, *My Years of Magical Thinking* (Mouse That Spins, 2017).
4. Alexander H. Tuttle, et. al., "Increasing placebo responses over time in US clinical trials of neuropathic pain." *PAIN* 156.12 (Dec. 2015): 2616–26. doi: 10.1097/j.pain.0000000000000333
5. Fabrizio Benedetti, Martina Amanzio, "The Placebo Response: How Words and Rituals Change the Patient's Brain," *Patient Education and Counseling* 84.3 (Sept. 2011): 413–19.
6. Donald D. Price, Damien G. Finniss, Fabrizio Benedetti, "A Comprehensive Review of the Placebo Effect: Recent Advances and Current Thought," *Annual Review of Psychology* 59 (2008): 565–90.
7. Sabine Vits, Manfred Schedlowski, "Learned Placebo Effects in the Immune System," *Zeitschrift für Psychologie* 222.3 (2014): 148–53.
8. Bruce Barrett et. al., "Placebo Effects and the Common Cold: A Randomized Controlled Trial," *Annals of Family Medicine* 9.4 (July/Aug. 2011): 312–22.
9. Alia Crum, William Corbin, et al., "Mind over Milkshakes: Mindsets, Not Just Nutrients, Determine the Ghrelin Response," *Health Psychology* 30.4 (2011): 424–29.
10. Winfried Häuser, Ernil Hansen, Paul Enck, "Nocebo Phenomena in Medicine: Their Relevance in Everyday Practice," *Deutches Artzblatt International* 109.26 (2012): 459–65.
11. Ibid. 12. Ibid.
13. Munya Andrews, *Journey into Dreamtime (Aboriginal Dreamtime)* (Ultimate World Publishing, 2019).
14. Amba Sepie, "More Than Stories, More than Myths: Animal/Human/Nature(s) in Traditional Ecological Worldviews," *Humanities* 6.4 (2017): 78; doi:10.3390/h6040078
15. Translated by J. Pedro Feliciano from the French and Greek: C.-E. Ruelle, ed. 1908; Hermès Trismégiste: Le Livre Sacré sur les Décans, pp. 247–77 in *Revue de philologie, de littérature et d'histoire anciennes* 32.
16. www.runesoup.com
17. Hilda Doolittle and Paul Bowles, *Notes on Thought and Vision* (City Lights, 2001).
18. Jess's field grimoire on Carrington is coming soon from Revelore Press.
19. For a more complete treatment of these amazing artists and their adventures, see: Stefan Van Raay, Joanna Moorhead, Teresa Arcq, Sharon-michi Kusunoki, Antonio Rivera, *Surreal Friends: Leonora Carrington, Remedios Varo, and Kati Horna* (Lund Humphries, 2010).
20. Meredith Derks, *Translating Magic: Remedios Varo's Visual Language*. MA Thesis. (University of Missouri-Kansas City, 2011).

Sign	Decan I	Decan II	Decan III
Cancer	Trunk	Lungs	Spleen
Leo	Heart	Upper Back	Liver
Virgo	Belly	Bowels	Navel
Libra	Buttocks & Rectum	Urethra, Bladder, & Urinary Tract	Anus
Scorpio	Clitoris & Penis	Genitals	Reproductive Organs
Sagittarius	Thigh Sores	Bones	Thighs
Capricorn	Kneecaps	Back of the Knees	Knees
Aquarius	Shins	Fatty Tissue of the Legs	Muscles of the Legs
Pisces	Abscesses of the Feet	Infections of the Feet	Feet
Aries	Head	Temples & Nose	Ears, Uvula, & Teeth
Taurus	Neck	Tonsils & Tongue	Mouth & Throat
Gemini	Shoulders	Arms	Hands

CANCER II: SOMACHALMAIS: LUNGS

Do you dare   linger   with me   the night

bear the waiting   fingertip   to lip   let   silence

like a walled garden   keep   absent within reach

hopes   and thrum   deep within

our edging   crepe myrtle skin   desire

to abandon all escape   to my arms   do you dare

come   gliding   Great Blue   biding   thunder

in its wake   to the wonder   of a mirrored lake

that holds tight   but never   takes the stars?

CANCER III: CHARMINE: SPLEEN

The self-same moon
swimming in my cup
held up in plate glass

skates the black lake
breaks into 1,000 pearls
strung in the wake of 2 bathing girls.

A mistake to see one w/out the other
the flipped coin's peak
counting drips & missing rain.

Nothing is extra that remains:
goosebumps, scales, blood stains
were in the water now & again after.

There is no moon without their laughter.

LEO I: ZOLOIAS: HEART

When
the   lion-headed
serpent   curls
around the ash tree
groaning like a galleon
in a gale, my son
it is already too late
cultivate a fencer's
hate long before
haughty eyes
the spine held straight
so the snake will know
you wait
awake
not to flinch but
snap
relaxed   at home
in the instant of death.
Show
only then your courage
your heart's   *lion*
blazoned on every pore   teeth bared
baleful roar

erupting in each breath
do not
forget who you are
one who spoeaks the divine name
who kindles
stars in your dreams
oh my son
then
and only
then when
it sees you stand
a hunter
will it kneel

LEO II: ZACHOR: UPPER BACK

Lift
your fists
raise the name
engraved cup revel
in your cuts let comrades
carry you on their shoulders
you've earned it this arch this
precarious balance between
whip & wand we call triumph
the exultation of all in one
keep it as long as you ought
for They will tell you Glory
Fades They will tell you This
Too Shall Pass & They are
right & yet the EAGLE & yet
the LION & yet the HAWK &
petrified rays of sunlight nothing lasts but everything is
forever & dying stars weep
iron birthing planetary cores
& again the iron surges forth
as granite lusting for the stars
what else to call this mystery
of pain & exultation but
victory or life or love or Isis
the wave crests yes oh yes
& the sea joys & remembers
I yet sing Alexandria that
sang the pharos that sang
the sun in the night & some
one will sing us one day with
the same tune in new skies

LEO III: FRICH: LIVER

come the flood come the fight come fire come fuckers
carrying torches come foe come fear come fate come
come and face us cowards we're waiting carrying
blood in our veins yet we hold fast to life we
LOVE it this moment this battle whatever
you got we are not inured we ENDURE
like crocodiles waiting maws agape
to grasp and tear elated we can
do this all day come break
your teeth on our bones
we're a wall   harder
than stone   we
hold fast we
know life
outlasts

REGULUS: RAPHAEL

What use is the Citadelle, San Souci palace,
your fifteen-foot portrait of Napoleon,
your stamped visage O HENRICUS
DEI GRATIA HAITI REX, when the stroke
hits, hemorrhaging blood like a hurricane,
your spine shivers like an earthquake,
and leaves you unsung and limping. No lion

lives long alone. Hunger thins tyrants
to skin and bone.
But together? They thrive.
Fat bellied. Bloody muzzled.
Lusty and alive the PRIDE

cannot be denied their roaring truth:
Suffering isn't found in MORE
but in hoarding, in holding on too long.

The slave whispering, "Sic Transit Gloria"
had it all wrong. It should have been
"This isn't about you."

VIRGO I: ZAMENDRES: BELLY

Pharaoh would know this hinged spine
& narrow head, the whine & delight
of both speed & sight
in the greyhound's light gallop. That's the history of it.
But history won't turn a hare. The hound
must dare to be where the prey
will go, to stare at what is not yet
there & so risk failure. To set
the best course takes a brave heart,
to know you cannot know from the start
what the end will be, like a beech tree
bending its roots through the rungs of the earth,
100 snake tongues seeking for the right way.
Themis, divine law, will have her say
in the shapes we play with, but none are ideal,
none fixed & sealed by a single hand.
Nothing stands still. The goalposts move
& with careful daring we improve, we make
the next impossible thing take shape.
We do not wait. We work. Looking fore & aft
drafting our hare's hooks & spins,
each miss a chance to begin again
the dance of the unknown known.
Students of what has been & what could be,
the prudent hazard life on what they see.

VIRGO II: MAGOIS: BOWELS

             dusky silt
brackish water   salt bleached
  dock   splintered ribs picked
  over   lilting
            macerated spine

caught in crescent moon filament O
virginia   you always knew
how   to   wait
steel   billed   ibis   fishing
  the shallows   long cane

 pole bending   with a guess
how many friends lost to you
  my river?   sunk in the marsh
or fiddler crab bait
      ain't so cute once you know
what they eat   chew

copper   gristle   saltwater
taffy & blood mixt
the estuary
         I drank   drowning
a taste can't never be got
            from out my mouth
I have no wish to die by
         fresh water
without oysters to bed down
safe harbored in my skull

VIRGO III: MICHULAIS: NAVEL

Taste of tobacco
                  lingers
burnt honey   finger to my lips
tips brush ginger gold
afternoon   sweeter for so soon lost
smoke tossed   breath   winding around
parking lot,
      dumpster rust,
             road sound
like   cedar resin   dipped linen   bound
              beauty
to the dead.   There's no sin
           in loving
the body,   our duty begins at the skin and extends   into stone.

Friends don't let friends die alone.

Sunset stains   holy crackling   cellophane
  & cigarette husks   leaf rot musk
          faint star promises
            be my sarcophagus
              please

    Seize

        me:
        all I ask is again

            forever.

LIBRA I: PSINEUS: BUTTOCKS & RECTUM

a swarm
and also a hush
of bees waiting a dance
a direction a time a spiral
music hanging a skyscraper
from a branch a skyscraper
and also glass elevators desks
trash cans love-notes sprinklers
steel beams letting the wind have
its way with them counterweighted
in tuned pendulum oscillations
little kisses of air

touch my back
just there
palm on my ribs
&
i'll follow you anywhere
so long as we keep dancing

LIBRA II: CHUSTHISIS: URETHRA, BLADDER, & URINARY TRACT

As horsehair catches catgut strings
aluminum rings with silt-rock scrape.
Echoes, tuning with marsh wrens, escape
the shore into the quiet flow of lake
skimming below the jon boat's skin
like waltzing heels float over sprung floor.
Wind feels its way over chest waders, blunted,
just as oxy shunted all to dull distance.
Touch we ever this existence? Full
disclosure, I so much hope it so.
That part of me goes with your ashes,
stashed among the fingerings and phrases
lingering in the dust of you, into the water
trussed with gull song & this day's sun
come so long a way for one final kiss.

LIBRA III: PSAMIATOIS: ANUS

20,000 ice crystals refract
    a coiling halo   for the moon
           unique
to each
      circling retina
              & photon

Firelight in python
scales loops
        the omphalos &
the oracle's
smoke-wreathed telling
   of a sure thing.

Always, a ring
          waiting the crowd to
clear space.
           A spotlight. A mirror.
Time to face that what cannot be
          escaped

must be owned.
            Mason marked
stones reveal

       there's no cathedral

just a spiralling
     garden of bones.

O friends   the wheel
  turns
    on what we do.
What's built on earth

           comes back to you.

SCORPIO I: NECBEUOS: CLITORIS & PENIS

Grand piano:

great black
       crab

88 ivory mandibles
& wire gullet

hammer lined stomach

crushing scales hidden
in air's polished
       carapace

No single sonata satisfies

the HUNGER

Feed it: hours.
Feed it: baseball diamonds & books.
Feed it: first loves, tearful farewells, & funerals

until it's big enough to be buried in

but, soft, why stop there?

Let ribs, let teeth fingers and spine
align the body gone

but longing 300 years
and every night

for one more song.

SCORPIO II: TURMANTIS: GENITALS

                Into true marriage
                      let us   admit
              some
                 impediment
for as the inked scorpion swims
the skin at the pleasure of rushing floods
of macrophages neither cast off nor destroyed

                so too the bodysurfer
              planes into the barrel

body taut to meet   the wave

pressing only velocity to fly
     his WHOLE WEIGHT

forward   free
in this suspended moment
were he
       for an instant
              to relent

and give himself to embracing sea
                      only crushing
                    ecstasy
                    a split skull
and the ocean would remain.

Likewise, the Atlantic would a desert make
if in love she never crashed again
curling UPWARD
      & UPWARD
            the titanic waterspout of love
                one
              great
              graceful
                 doom.

As these
      the heart.

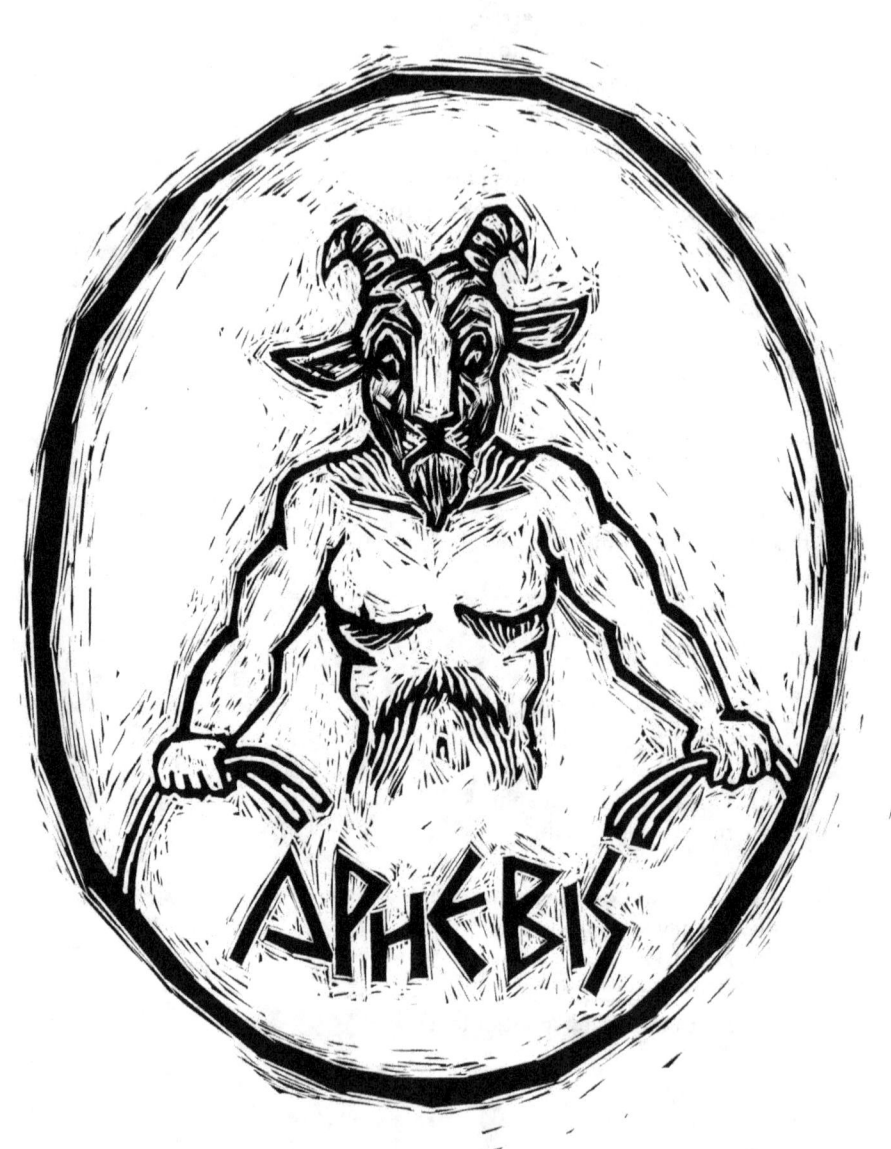

SCORPIO III: PSERMES: REPRODUCTIVE ORGANS

In the chess hustler's outstretched hand,
the wringing of a wedding band,
the grand gesture on bended knee,
a line to sign & offered key,

the purling sea & small ship's lure,
the poison promised as a cure,
the sure thing bar napkin ground floor,
the never-before-seen blue door,

and more, wait: chances to be plucked,
prized won or damnation ducked
with lucked into perfect measure.
The instant of choice the treasure.

But pleasure dulls. The aftermath—
goat horns, blood smear, strewn red cup path—
offers a quiet choice: be done
or be chained to the paling fun.

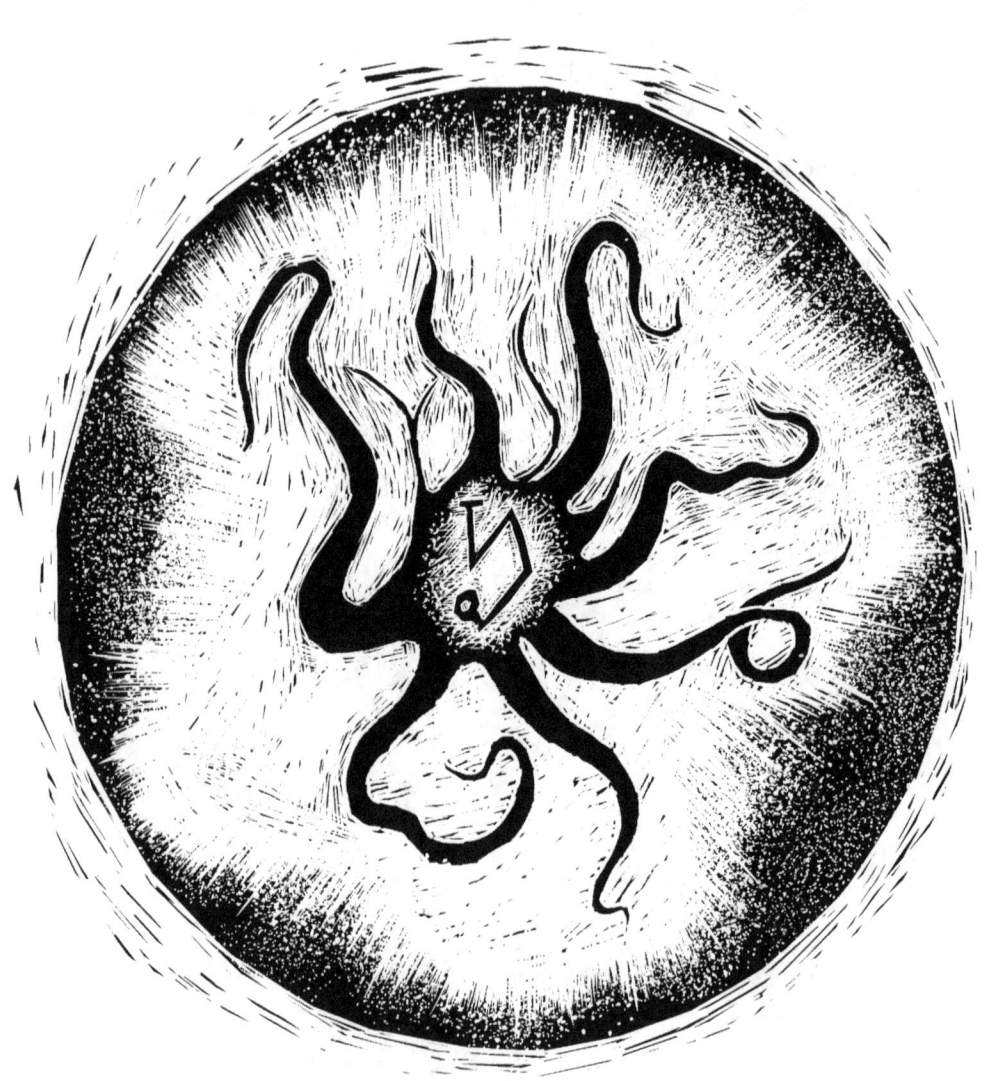

ANTARES: URIEL

Tell me, angel. What am I
to know of alchemy?

Pure water broken out of poison
rain with charcoal and time.

Sweat labor exchanged
for sunflowers and birdsong.

Straining blue velvet cloud banks
released by scalpel lightning.

Shoals of hope and pain
in an instant become a child.

Written on my palm and yours
energy changed into matter and speed

for your every breath is gold.
Nothing is lost but arranged

by desire. Every day the world
gains a lover, sheds its velvet

unrestrained to rut and join
together what is never asunder.

This sacred ache sustains
your proton communion kiss

your needy fusion hearts,
your changing perfect beauty.

This you are to know of alchemy.

SAGITTARIUS I: CLINOTHOIS: THIGH SORES

straight razor singing	needle floating north	the *jian* aches in its rosewood case
O! O! just	the slightest touch	hold frame: not your partner
firefly yet living	in yr hollowed hand	pull and release
hot buzzing arrow	darting silver fish	cut and cut again
small mouths	small price	for balance
wrapped in ray skin	fit out with love	and german silver

SAGITTARIUS II: THURSOIS: BONES

Reduction: the bonesetter's art:
to guide back into place.
How lovely.
To think, with a well placed blow and twist,
all the pins will tumble into place:
that hands can move like tugboats
through a deep fog, shepherding strays
back into the channel by feel
and true memory of the curve of an embankment,
by soundings and secrets.
How lovely, how absurd
this spectrum of touch,
this patient violence,
three nails shivering in two beams
frame a scaffold
where what was broken
may yet knit. A carpenter's eye knows:
This house has good bones,
there's years in'er yet.

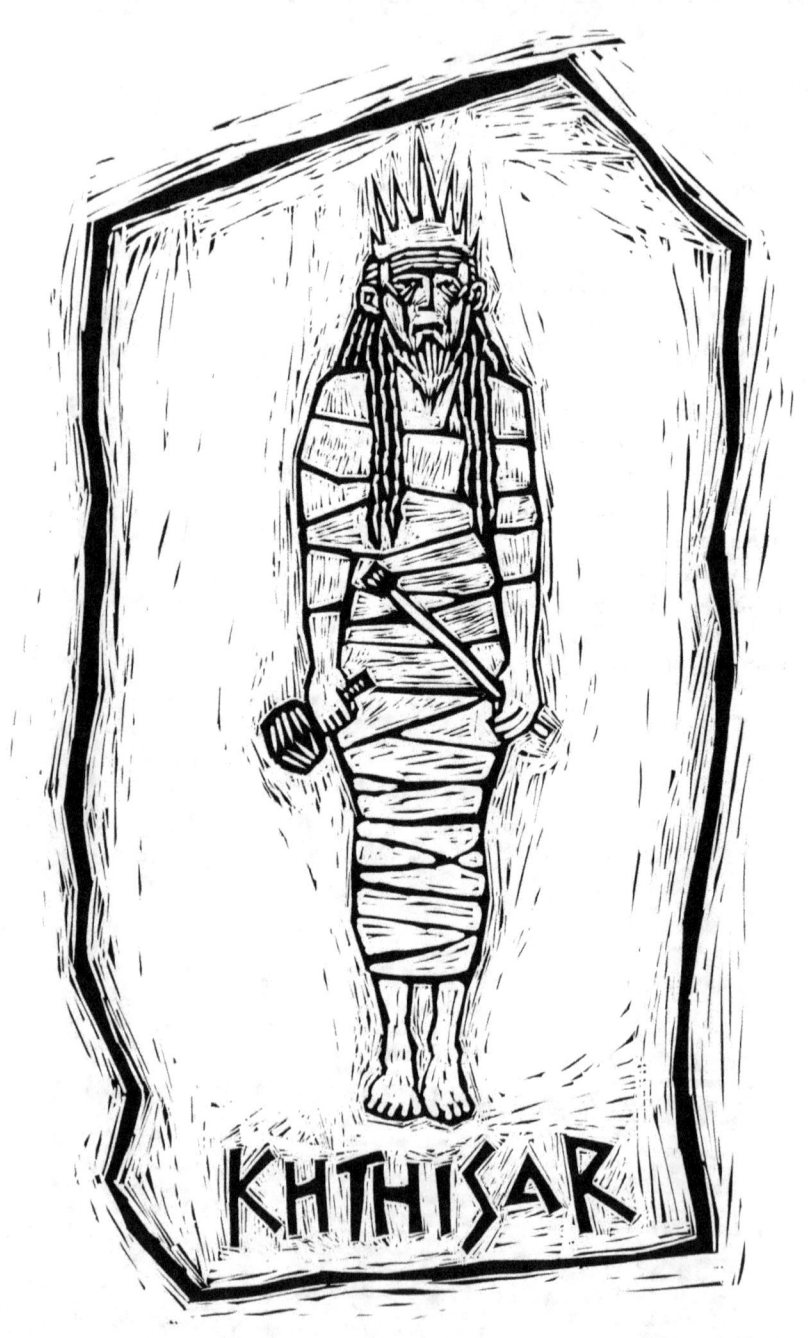

SAGITTARIUS III: RENETHIS: THIGHS

From the spindle of your spine radiate
bifurcating lines, a forest of paths
through which SHE coils, rust-dressed Ananke,
mother to all: abjured crowns, backseat lust,
drowned galleons, vast deserts of dust, night —
whom the gods fear to fight: Necessity.
Steer how ye list, she is the sea. Her gifts,
this bony zodiac, this compass, sift
wishes and lift up what can yet be done.
One move will set the board, eliminate
a hoard of hopes, just the sacrifice left:
rusting back, black lung, the sluggish office
suicide. Trust me, young one. she says That's the play.
Give it all, gladly, for love: deny lives
to live, happy and toughened by true care.
Dare to give enough and don't turn away:
though only enough and no more.

CAPRICORN I: RENEPOIS: KNEECAPS

                    Look, he said,
                            so I looked
                            and I saw:

                            Nailed to the piling
                a decapitated cottonmouth
              coiling the creosoted wood,
      its dark body (a batted eyelash)

                brushing the water
                        like the edge of a bridged card
                                or smoke on the lip of a pistol.

                    and I felt
                in me
        the same curling need
    to break free of the hand that held me.

                        Look, he said.
                        It thinks it's alive.

                        Isn't that funny.

CAPRICORN II: MANETHOIS: BACK OF THE KNEES

The bull
        rises
              as the light glints off
his heavy horns, his double bladed axes:

tugged
      by the sun
           (tho HE is weightless)
      to the delicious infinity of grass
                  snuffling
                      gently
                  its sweet
                            wet enticements.

We die so many times before we're through.

To it then, with small tugs —
      a way begins
           via negativa, and the teeth,
                        the stolid neck,
start

the course, plowed
      into a path
           by the scarab-colored hooves,
           to make of pasture
              a lawn
              to set
a limit
     and create
a kingdom.

He cares for nothing else. The paddock gate
            is always
            open. Yet
            with each
            stamp
            and tail whip, he is
at home in   any   corner of the world
where he may work in his medium.

CAPRICORN III: MARXOIS: KNEES

Comes now the corn pest,
creaky singer, in oil slick iridescence clothed

cackler, counterpuncher,
the grackle groks the timing,

the mousetrap chink/crack,
not one-two but single snap

to snatch the worm
to sack the city.

The audacity of nope
that's mine.

Kingly virtue.

Outcomes should not concern us.
Courage captures the opportunity

stands to cut the arrow
crashes through factory gates

clasps the offered hand,
bands together to keep the line,

as the blitzing cataract
refracts the light into a bow

and catches the sun unawares:
creates the lucky break,

the unlooked for, the eucatastrophe.

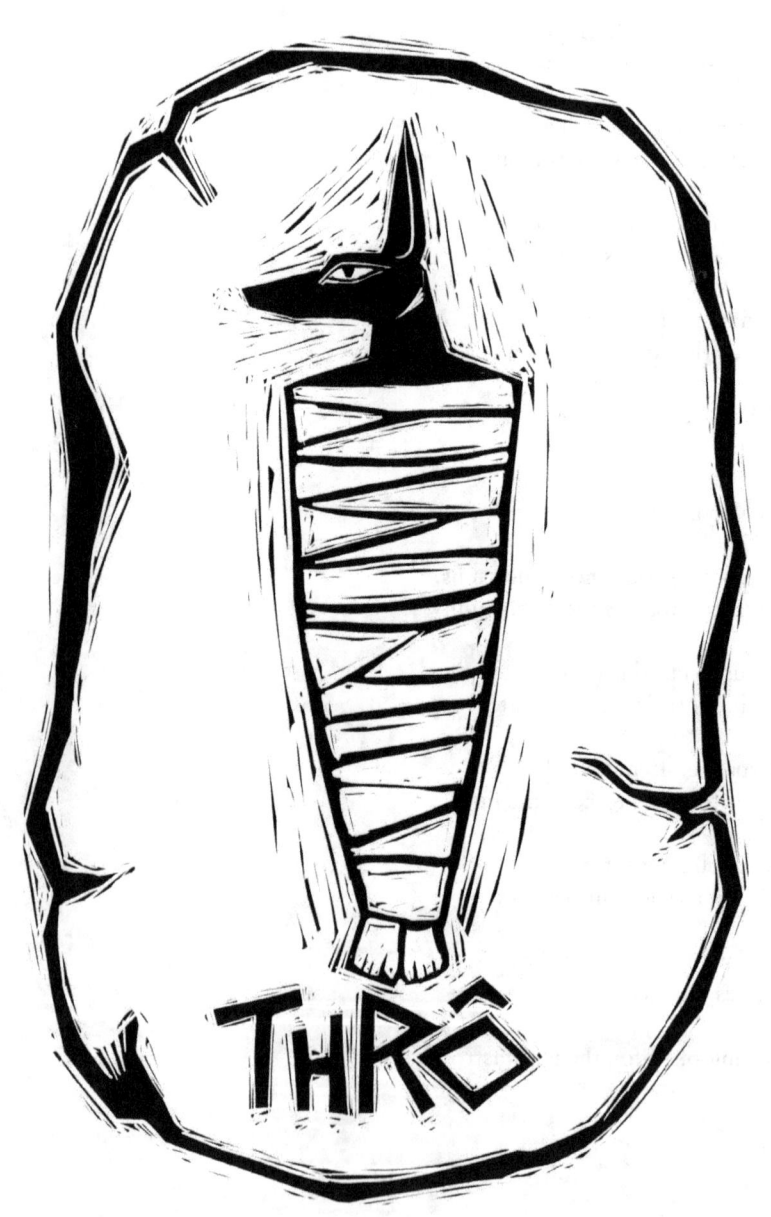

AQUARIUS I: ULARIS: SHINS

In remembrance of
frosted beech forests
wild   ginger yellow   eyes
just   beyond   the fire
smoking meat
            an offering
in no man's land

In remembrance of
the long testing of the herd
sharp copper
       proof of weakness
from each,
    their chosen part
to each,
      their rightful share
custom
shaping even the body
into something new

In remembrance of this
I take the wet tennis ball
and I throw it.

AQUARIUS II: LUXOIS:
FATTY TISSUE OF THE LEGS

go forth by night go
forth bearing your auburn grandmother's
silver basin & 3 hawthorn
branches bury into the creekbed
knee deep between them bind
the moon with running water
wait because this is work
begin the song of Him
Who Lives by Hearts behold
the face you fear break
now drink deep how bright
your skin here beneath cold
water beyond black space of
all beginnings bare your teeth
your fists unbridle bring back
the basin love when you're
done & tell me whose
mask was betrayed to you

AQUARIUS III: CRAUXES: LEG MUSCLES

I put it to you
     philosophy provides nothing so pure
as a piebald pitbull
         pulling week old ham
from a garbage pail
crowned in wrappers
and accompanied by crashing pans.
Keep it simple. Parrot no master.
     Sleep together. Pet your friends.
Snap your foes. Whoop
     at the moon & prepare ye
the path that passes all understanding

For all is already perished and passed away.

FOMALHAUT: GABRIEL

As he stared into Balikili Gol, the reflecting pool
of Atargartis, where the sacred fish
swim among the stars each night
and are stars reflecting to each other
in one constellated net for beauty,
the Angel Gabriel realized something
I already knew 6,000 years later
seeing my face in the warm brown earth
and green glass-trapped sunlight
of my beloved's eyes.
You shall have no other gods before Love.
And the longing you feel
to press your heart to their heart
and admit you would dive into a wild sea
to touch them again for an instant
is the only gospel worth living for.

PISCES I: FAMBRAIS: ABSCESSES OF THE FEET

Even here   on this half snowed sunny quad

      I am sunk
      six feet
just deep enough to drown in
                one more failed magician in a water tank

at 17 I got it,
        water wrapped and staring

up
at a world just
        beyond my reach
sunlight   slurred by pine needles &   2 extra inches
    and on that firmament no star chart
but the veins of the birth caul
            the vellum mapped by my heartbeats
my breaths
always finite now numbered
            strangely no more immortal than a marble face
cracked on the seabed below Knossos

        All water is endless when you've
        nowhere else to go

but all that brought me here
        brought me out:
        friendship, small acts of daring—
and I emerged again, buried in water yet risen
to walk in the newness of life.

        This, of course, but the first remembered
of many drownings.

PISCES II: FLUGMOIS: INFECTIONS OF THE FEET

```
Pretty         like skimming      thank Venus         taught me
     & muscled           dolphins            so they          the net
the sand       the sea if ye       and the crowd       crashing
     safer than         kept yr feet          voices          down
the colonnade   to be heard       a wish and see      death was
     they came          to call out         it done          a lure
but courage    a decade in        they set me some    farmboy as
     set the hook       blood adorned       unscarred       secutor
the sheep had   his betrothed     I dragged it out    of him
     a bad year         now too rich        took care       my teeth
never scraped   he had no legs    like a sturgeon     I came close
     his neck but      I had to haul him    but when        dropped
my elbow like   he took it        his broadleafed dagger   he butted me
     this and ha!       like we agreed       cut above my eyes   a RAM
and I lifted my    mercy        what the people most wish   the coins were
     finger             mercy                to give         scales
in the sunlight    in the sand     I was more lovely     brought splendor
     soft rain         paid his debts       and the crowd    home
kissed wishes    bright treasure    a story to tell     before sons
     in the fountain    in the depths      around fires    must sleep
```

PISCES III: PIASTRIS: THE FEET

Cold sunlight and road salt (March, Chelsea).
Breath mist mixing with exhaust, sharp copper
scent
        of
                blood, pooling
                on the sidewalk
rippling black ice and steam rising like a coiling racer.

Two ghosts, knife handed, screaming into the wind
come together, pull apart, and come together again.

Now mingled here at the death of the year
with the gall of the city. Nothing left but to name the loss
and hope for better — to yearn for it —
but the crocuses, expected,
are as yet
beyond the palisades of spring.

ARIES I: AULATHAMUS: THE HEAD

and am I not also spring
waiting, here, in the dark,
black dirt, rich in gems,
rich in wanting, impatient
as the thaw draws the ache
from my stones, o grinding
of frost heaves how long
must I dream of seed
planted in my chest to pull
at once for water and sky
take from me my rib
for your trees my spine
for your cowslips, fingernail
irises, teeth lilies, and shin orchid
all all I will bear whatever you wish
for the song of wind in your hair
a single sun lipped kiss
will keep me tangled in your roots
my love, don't forget I too
have waited the winter

ARIES II: SABAOTH: TEMPLES & NOSE

And then QUICK! the sap
      bloods the soil
with colored
      pinpricks dazzling
      toxins, the daffodil
crown of the lady of hosts
      rising
      unannounced
bursting from the dead earth in terrible stain
      scarlet tongue lolling
                  back
arched ecstasy   echoing
      her earthquake.
      O queen unquelled by winter
QUICKEN ME
that the swift hart not outstrip my fangs
that my paws find purchase across the hoof sparked stone
that I not grow faint before my foe.
      Lady
      so long asleep
now that your blades raise & all must
      wear your colors or perish
let the QUICK coming from the dead never falter,
let your reign
      ruthless
      & unrestrained
course our veins in
      shud
         der
            ing
               bliss
this
new spring,
these
fresh stars.

ARIES III: DISORNAFIAS: EARS, UVULA, & TEETH

The belle's art of backleading
through a waltzing jungle

softly, softly, the fingertips pet
the scales, lamplight on vellum,

the gold chevrons twitch, he rears,
but she stays in frame, keeps contact

keeps close to the cobra and to death
her dress flaps and he snaps

the air, and again, she caresses his neck,
come darling, come sweetness, she sings

he forgets she was not always there,
perhaps she was, perhaps she is,

her hand on his throat, she lowers her mouth
star perfume, falling light,

to his, one kiss — he grants it
of course, this is all he wanted

everything led to this, naturally.
Naturally, he would. Of course. Of course.

TAURUS I: JAUS: THE NECK

First, the sunflower,
spinning within ultraviolet ribbons
to face the sun, roots beating deeper,
stem stretching to meet
warmth, to arrive in perfect time,
light drunk and blind

and then, the pineal gland
grandmaster sleep, nightflowering primrose
photon shy third eye closing
at electric signal fires along the great wall of nerves
and with it the gate of dream,

map this our fractal world
our fluttering image held taut
in each perspective.

So it has always been true
the Charities are at least three
and I name them
perceive
receive
transmit
and their winding dance
I call GRACE for lack of a more perfect word.

TAURUS II: SARNATOIS: TONSILS & TONGUE

In moonlight, in a flock of apple blossoms,
of red clay she made her Adam,
                          her first, her only.
Petals stuck to his curling beard.

Look at you,
       old man,
she said.

In moonlight, with her hands, she made him,
with her spit and breath, with laughter and sweat along his shoulders.

Too big, her sisters said.
His teeth are like boulders.

Too big, her mothers said.
You'll never feed him.

Too big, said her most & least
favorite aunts. How will you keep him?

But he woke in rain and she shushed him.
She traced his name on his ribs with dittany, milk, and honey.

He walked
       a head taller than the trees
                     and carried her,
                                and asked questions.
What is that serpent?
                   The Long River.
How long have you been here?
                        Always and a day.

Why did you make me?
                   To see the stars in your eyes.
                   Look up.
                   Look up, sweeting.
Then he would sigh,
the night air rushing through his chest like an unseen ocean
and at last
she would sleep.

TAURUS III: ROMENUR: MOUTH & THROAT

You make it too hard to pray
say nothing
                    get down on all fours
course the hare   quiver back
the tracks are burning embers
holy pine cones   yearning   bright

in smoke adorning night

remember, you were born

with a shining crown of thorns
you were born
                lining your cheeks with pearls
you were born
          with curls of myrrh
stirring your breath
                you were stained glass
you were
        and will be again

CAPUT ALGOL: THE DEMON'S HEAD

Red hot muzzle glow
an instant before a revolver
in a woman's hand
returns the favor
and the Emperor's spotless uniform
is a white flag in a pile of corpses.

Viva the return to heads rolling
and needles knitting,
the crones chant "such pretty CURLS
what a fine scarf for my girl not yet 10,"
the basket soaks red.

Judith's handmaid carries Holofernes like laundry:
just another spot scrubbed out
with a little elbow grease.

Her chariot wheels running smooth
on the fat of her enemies, Boudica
circles every city waiting to tattoo
a line of ash in the heart of each man.

And so on and so on
back to the beginning. To firehaired,
firstborn, unbowed Lilith, teaching
her daughters the screech owl song
to turn a heart to stone:

"I brought you into this world. I will take you out."

ALDEBARAN: MICHAEL

Handle the bull with a staff and take no chances

A tornado trapped in a solid ton
of muscle and menace, a maelstrom,
the fight for freedom made flesh,
a bellowing bucking battering ram,
a blood-eyed beauty that will end you.

You can't outmuscle the bull. Make other plans.
Give in to gravity; go along for the ride.
Patience. Prayer. Put aside
everything but the unsung excellence
of this deadly dance: dare to follow

his lead. Learn to love
sweet grass, soft nosed cows,
the sweltering stillness of the sun
carried calmly in his horns across
the wheat field, the furrows filling
with rain, ever ready rage,
and pure lust for power. The present
where all is breath and backbreaking spin.

The sweet stillness only in the eye of the storm
where eight seconds is a seam of eternity.
Love and let go of your short life
if you want to hold on.

The gentle bull, not the vicious one, most often
kills or maims his keeper.

GEMINI I:
MANUCHOS:
SHOULDERS

A net worked
to catch light

a single wire cut
then twisted

intersecting
grains of silver

to call this
distraction

interference
to forget

the beaded sea
falling from her hair

to your lips the moon
over wheatfields

is some kind of sacrilege
it matters

what you think
it is a chain

linked a fence
a shirt a necklace

from which we
pendant in space

anchor splendor
& 10,000 things beside

GEMINI II: SAMUROIS: ARMS

The path is not a razor's edge

not wedged between mountains
nor hedged with crosses

marked out in losses
barked at by unfed dogs

nor red with slain buddhas.
Not even death, nor the rain

but the buoyant line of breath
suspended between the wine glass

and the fine deep night.
Your birthright, my son.

This strange letting go we call delight.

GEMINI III: AZUEL: HANDS

To refuse to choose is also a choice
silence the roaring voice of the unsaid

the weight of the undead waiting to be
cannot be born without the great gift

the hand lifting a sailor from the sea
does not set the yet unsaved out to drift

unbraved unrisked unlived and unseen
is a mean wish. We dream what we can

and set from dark to dark a shining span.

CANCER I: SOTHEIR: SIDES OF THE TRUNK

Against opinion, the world does not end
in fire or ice, though the sun IS swaddled
by a great serpent, stowed in her soft mouth
and carried safe through the void gate of night.

There is only one, after all. One light,
one garden, one bright-eyed peacock angel,
one pharoah with many fames bound wire tight
to the stars serving the one same people.

It has a name: this spiral, this egg. Not
"first" nor "lust" nor "chaos" nor "mist" nor "fog"
but TRUST.
      Only trust, that nothing is missed
that future children know us already—

as we carry them wrapped within our hearts.

A WHEEL OF SMALL GODS

was typeset in Sabon, a font designed by Jan Tschichold between 1964–1967 and based on typefaces by Claude Garamond. This book was first printed in MMXXII with a companion divination deck, *THE ORACLE OF DECANS*.

www.revelore.press/wosg